12 ENTERTAINERS
WHO CHANGED THE WORLD

by M. J. York

STORY LIBRARY

www.12StoryLibrary.com

Copyright © 2016 by Peterson Publishing Company, North Mankato, MN 56003. All rights
reserved. No part of this book may be reproduced or utilized in any form or by any means
without written permission from the publisher.

12-Story Library is an imprint of Peterson Publishing Company and Press Room Editions.

Produced for 12-Story Library by Red Line Editorial

ISBN
978-1-63235-147-0 (hardcover)
978-1-63235-188-3 (paperback)
978-1-62143-240-1 (hosted ebook)

Library of Congress Control Number: 2015934290

Printed in the United States of America
Mankato, MN
June, 2015

Go beyond the book. Get free,
up-to-date content on this topic
at 12StoryLibrary.com.

TABLE OF CONTENTS

BEYONCÉ EMPOWERS WOMEN AND GIRLS

Beyoncé is a global superstar. She was born on September 4, 1981, in Houston, Texas. Beyoncé Giselle Knowles-Carter became a performer at an early age. As a teenager, Beyoncé and three friends started Destiny's Child, an R&B singing group. The group saw a lot of success before breaking apart in 2005.

Beyoncé continued working in the entertainment industry after Destiny's Child. She has created seven solo albums. She has also appeared in several movies, including *Dreamgirls* and *Cadillac Records*. These albums and movies earned Beyoncé many different awards. She is the single most nominated woman in Grammy history.

While not working in the studio or on a movie set, Beyoncé spends a lot of time giving to various charities. Beyoncé and fellow Destiny's Child member and friend Kelly Rowland founded the Survivor Foundation. They

Beyoncé holds the three Grammies she won at the 57th Grammy Awards in 2015.

created it after Hurricane Katrina in 2005. This foundation provides assistance, education, and support to those suffering hard times.

Providing food to the hungry is an important part of Beyoncé's charity work. She was an ambassador for the 2005 World Children's Day. She held food drives before her concerts in 2006. The food went to Hurricane Katrina victims. Beyoncé has also partnered with

Beyoncé speaks at a press conference for Feeding America in June 2009.

Feeding America and the Houston Food Bank. She also works with the Global Food Banking Network and the Bread of Life Miss a Meal program.

Another cause that is important to Beyoncé is female empowerment. In 2013, Beyoncé helped co-found the Chime for Change program. Chime for Change raises money and awareness for females around the world. The organization has started more than 400 projects in 86 countries. Beyoncé has lent her musical talent and donated $500,000 to the organization.

52

Number of Grammy nominations Beyoncé received during her career, as of spring 2015.

- Beyoncé is an award-winning musician and actor.
- Her songs and charity work include teaching young girls about empowerment.
- Beyoncé also works to end hunger.

2

BONO OPENS OUR EYES TO GLOBAL POVERTY

Singer Bono is known for both political songs and political action. The rocker was born in 1960 in Dublin, Ireland. His real name is Paul David Hewson. He got the nickname Bono in high school. It is short for Bono Vox, Latin for "good voice." His

band U2 formed in 1976. Bono was just 16 years old.

Many of U2's early hits had social, spiritual, or political messages. One famous example is "Sunday, Bloody Sunday." It pled for peace in Ireland. It describes violent

Bono is a rocker who also works to end poverty and improve health care worldwide.

events that happened in Ireland on January 30, 1972. U2 and Bono began performing in charity aid concerts in the 1980s.

Since the 1990s, Bono has worked with many charities. He works tirelessly to improve human health and end poverty. Many of his efforts focus on Africa. He meets with world leaders. Many of these leaders' countries have loaned money to poorer nations. Bono urges them not to require the poorer nations to pay them back. He says the poorer countries could use the money to educate and provide health care to children.

Bono cofounded the organizations ONE and Product (RED). ONE helps 11 existing aid organizations work

22
Number of Grammies U2 won between 1987 and 2014.

- Bono is the front man of the successful Irish rock band U2.
- He raises awareness for health programs, especially in Africa.
- He works to reduce poverty in African countries.

together. It asks governments to send money where people need it most. Through Product (RED), companies sell products and donate part of the sales. The money helps fight AIDS and other diseases.

Bono at a ONE campaign event in Germany in 2013

GEORGE CLOONEY SPEAKS AGAINST GENOCIDE

George Clooney is an Academy Award–winning actor and producer. He was born in 1961 in Kentucky. In the early 1980s, he moved to Los Angeles, California. His aunt, Rosemary Clooney, was a movie star. But George's career started slowly. He had only small roles until 1994. That year, he got a lead role on TV's *ER*. After that, he quickly landed movie roles that made him famous. He has won numerous awards, including two Oscars.

Since becoming famous, Clooney has raised his voice for humanitarian causes. He works to end genocide in the Darfur region of Sudan. The government and the region's tribes have been fighting since 2003. By 2014, at least 400,000 people were dead. At least 2.5 million people became refugees. In 2010, Clooney helped launch the Satellite Sentinel Project. Satellites take images of Sudan from space. They show destruction and signs of coming violence. The images help show the world genocide is happening in Sudan.

Clooney is an award-winning actor.

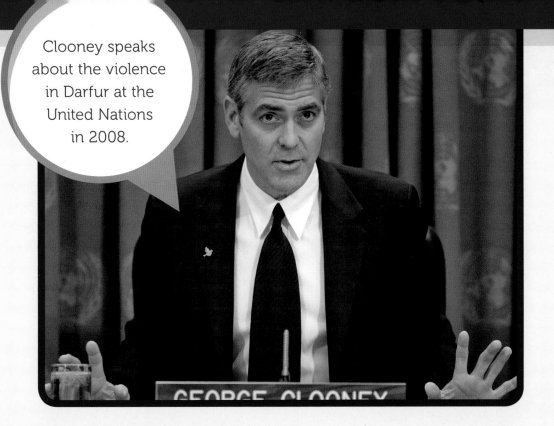

Clooney speaks about the violence in Darfur at the United Nations in 2008.

In 2007, Clooney cofounded the organization Not on Our Watch. Don Cheadle, Matt Damon, and Brad Pitt helped found it, too. The actors worked together on the movie *Ocean's Eleven*. Clooney visits war-torn regions. He raises money and speaks to world leaders.

6
Years Clooney served as a United Nations Messenger for Peace.

- Clooney is an award-winning actor, director, screenwriter, and producer.
- He works to end genocide in Darfur.
- He also raises money for disaster relief and to end poverty.

THINK ABOUT IT

How does George Clooney help refugees in Sudan? What are some ways other people are working to help? What could you or your class do? Find articles or research online to learn more.

ELLEN DEGENERES GETS VIEWERS TO CARE

Ellen DeGeneres is an influential daytime TV host. She has hosted the *Ellen DeGeneres Show* for more than a decade. She is also a leader in charitable giving. DeGeneres was born in Louisiana in 1958. She started her career as a stand-up comedian. She had a successful sitcom from 1994 to 1998.

DeGeneres broke barriers in society and made gay rights issues more

ELLEN LOVES ANIMALS

DeGeneres is known for her commitment to animal welfare and rights. She owns the pet food company Halo. The company gave 1 million meals to animal shelters in 2010. DeGeneres does not eat meat or animal products. She helps groups such as Farm Sanctuary rescue suffering or abused animals. She works with the Humane Society of the United States. She helps the society find homes for animals.

DeGeneres uses her fame to support various causes.

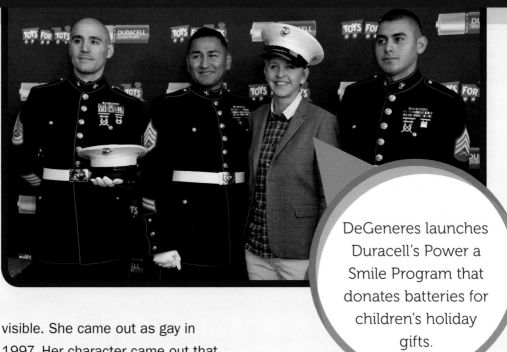

DeGeneres launches Duracell's Power a Smile Program that donates batteries for children's holiday gifts.

visible. She came out as gay in 1997. Her character came out that year on her sitcom, too. She was the first gay lead character on TV. In real life, DeGeneres married actress Portia de Rossi in 2008.

45

Number of charities DeGeneres supports.

- DeGeneres is a comedian and award-winning talk show host.
- She was one of the first actors to come out as gay and played TV's first gay lead character.
- She speaks up for gay rights, animal rights, and humanitarian causes.

DeGeneres has hosted the *Ellen DeGeneres Show* since 2003. She is likeable and funny. She is known for her goofy dance moves. DeGeneres encourages viewers to support social, health, and environmental groups. Some causes include Stand Up to Cancer and the anti-bullying organization the Trevor Project. She also does work for the American Red Cross. She launched the Small Change Campaign with actor Ben Affleck. The campaign supports Second Harvest. The charity collects and gives out food to organizations. The food is used to feed hungry Americans.

LEONARDO DICAPRIO BRINGS ATTENTION TO CLIMATE CHANGE

Actor Leonardo DiCaprio is a big name in show business. Outside Hollywood, he donates his time and money to help the environment. DiCaprio was born in 1974 in Los Angeles, California. He started landing small TV roles as a teenager. In his early movie roles, he played troubled, complex characters. His performances earned

In 2014, DiCaprio was named a UN Messenger of Peace.

$2 million

Amount the Leonardo DiCaprio Foundation gave to stop overfishing in 2014.

- DiCaprio is an Academy Award–nominated actor.
- He works to help the environment and stop climate change.
- He also does humanitarian work.

good reviews. In 1997, *Titanic* shot DiCaprio to superstardom. Since then, he has starred in several movies. In 2013, he gave an award-winning performance in *The Wolf of Wall Street*. It also gained him his fourth Academy Award nomination.

DiCaprio started the Leonardo DiCaprio Foundation in 1998. The foundation fights against climate change. It gives money to other groups that work for the environment. It spends millions of dollars on small projects. For example, the foundation has helped protect tigers in Nepal. It has also created ocean sanctuaries.

DiCaprio helps steer the world's leading conservation organization. He is on the board of directors of the World Wildlife Fund. In 2014, the United Nations (UN) recognized DiCaprio's environmental work. It named him a UN Messenger of Peace. As a messenger, he helps others understand the environmental work the UN does.

FILMS FOR ACTION

DiCaprio also uses his fame to raise awareness. In 2007, he wrote and narrated *The Eleventh Hour*. It is a documentary about climate change. The film explains threats to the environment. It asks viewers to help. In 2014 and 2015, he released short films calling for action on climate change. He narrated and helped fund the series.

BOB HOPE ENTERTAINS THE TROOPS

Comedian Bob Hope was known for his quick wit and one-liner jokes. He hosted the Academy Awards 19 times. His style of stand-up inspires comics today. His greatest legacy, though, is his work with the US military. He spent decades hosting overseas tours entertaining US troops.

Hope was born in 1903 in England. His family moved to Cleveland, Ohio, when he was four years old. He got his start on Broadway and on the radio in the 1920s. He broke into film in the 1930s.

Hope traveled around the world performing at USO shows.

In the 1940s, Hope brought a stage show around the world. He visited military bases and war zones during World War II (1939–1945). His work lifted the spirits of soldiers serving overseas. He worked with the United Service Organizations (USO). The USO sends entertainers to visit the troops. It sponsors other programs to help troop morale. Hope entertained troops in every US conflict through the Persian Gulf War in 1990. Hope died in 2003 at age 100.

5

Number of Academy Awards Hope won for his work in film and for humanitarian causes.

- Hope was a comedian on radio, stage, film, and TV.
- He raised troop morale in war zones for five decades.
- He is the only person ever to be named an honorary veteran.

HOPE'S LEGACY

In 1997, Congress named Hope an honorary veteran. He is the only person ever to receive this honor. In addition, he received more than 50 honorary degrees from universities. He won an award from President Bill Clinton. He earned a British knighthood. The USNS *Bob Hope* transport ship is named after him.

In 1978, Hope was honored in Washington, DC.

ANGELINA JOLIE BRINGS HOPE TO REFUGEES

Angelina Jolie says filming a movie in Cambodia opened her eyes to human suffering. It led the actress to begin humanitarian work. Today, she works for human rights worldwide.

Jolie was born in Los Angeles, California, in 1975. She is the daughter of famous actor Jon Voight. Her own acting career took off in the late 1990s. She won an Academy Award in 2000 for her role in *Girl, Interrupted*. Her career has mixed challenging dramatic roles with action

Jolie speaks at the 2013 Global Summit on Ending Sexual Violence.

A CHARITABLE FAMILY

Jolie married actor Brad Pitt in 2014. The couple supports many causes. They have six children whom they are raising as activists. Their son Maddox was born in 2001 in Cambodia. Jolie adopted him in 2002. She started a foundation in his name in 2003. The Maddox Jolie-Pitt foundation works to save the environment in Cambodia.

Chechen refugees speak with Jolie in 2003.

flicks. She directed her first full-length film in 2011.

But Jolie also works for numerous human rights causes. She has

a close relationship with the UN. She has donated more than $5 million to the UN since 2001. She began working with the UN High Commissioner for Refugees that year. She became a UN Goodwill Ambassador in 2001, too. Jolie visits refugee camps around the world. She became a UN Special Envoy in 2012. As a special envoy, she asks world leaders for support for refugees. She also raises money and awareness for many humanitarian causes. One cause is ending sexual violence in war zones.

40

Number of field missions to help refugees Jolie has taken for the UN.

- Jolie is an Academy Award–winning actress.
- She works with the UN to aid refugees worldwide.
- She also works to end sexual violence.

JOHN LENNON INSPIRES PEACE FOR GENERATIONS

John Lennon was one of the most influential songwriters in history. He was born in Liverpool, England, in 1940. During the 1960s, he wrote dozens of hit songs with songwriting partner Paul McCartney. They wrote for their band, the Beatles. The Beatles brought new techniques and

Lennon and Yoko Ono during their Bed-In

1

Rank Lennon's solo album *Imagine* reached on the Billboard music charts.

- Lennon was a Rock and Roll Hall of Fame member and chart-topping artist.
- He wrote songs about love and peace.
- He worked for peace during the Vietnam War, and his songs continue to inspire people today.

THINK ABOUT IT

Do you think songs can motivate people and politicians to change things? Why or why not? Find articles or research online to support your opinion.

new ideas to pop music. They have influenced artists of every decade since.

Lennon used his fame to work for world peace. Lennon sang about love and peace during the Vietnam War (1955–1975). Songs such as "All You Need Is Love" and "Imagine" spoke to a generation. With his wife Yoko Ono, Lennon staged a peaceful protest. They called it a Bed-In. It happened on the couple's honeymoon in 1969. They invited reporters into their hotel room. They used the media attention to call for world peace.

A fan suffering from a mental disability shot and killed Lennon in 1980. But Lennon's songs and message live on. His music inspired Americans after the terror attacks of September 11, 2001. A concert honored Lennon's music and desire for peace. It also raised money to care for victims of the attacks. In 2014, humanitarian group UNICEF used Lennon's song "Imagine" to raise money. It asked people to upload their versions of "Imagine" for its #IMAGINE campaign. Many celebrities performed the song, too. The campaign raised money to help children around the world.

EVA LONGORIA HELPS LATINAS

Eva Longoria became famous for her role as Gabrielle Solis on the TV show *Desperate Housewives*. She has used her fame to change the world. The Texas native helped reelect President Barack Obama in 2012.

Longoria was born in Corpus Christi, Texas, in 1975. She is Mexican American. Longoria's focus is Latino issues. Changing US immigration policies is especially important to her. She helped start the Latino Victory Project. The group encourages Latinos to vote. She spoke before Congress about helping Latina businesses grow. She has also made two documentary films about farmworkers.

Longoria created the Eva Longoria Foundation. It helps

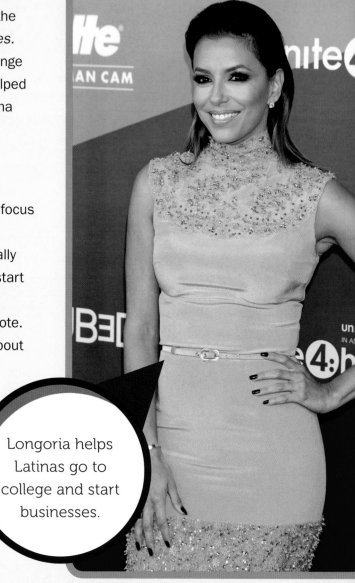

Longoria helps Latinas go to college and start businesses.

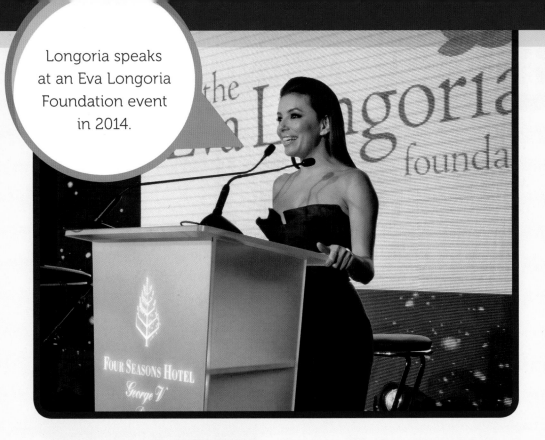

90

Number of Latina business owners who received loans from the Eva Longoria Foundation between 2013 and spring 2015.

- Longoria is a TV and film actress.
- She works on Latino issues, including education and immigration reform.
- Her Eva's Heroes group helps children with special needs.

Latina students go to college. It also funds new Latina businesses. She cofounded Eva's Heroes. This group helps children with special needs lead richer lives. The cause is near to Longoria's heart because her sister has an intellectual disability.

THINK ABOUT IT

What causes are important to you? Why do you care about them? Would you donate your time to help? Would you give money?

21

10

MADONNA RAISES MALAWI

Madonna is a music superstar. She was born Madonna Louise Ciccone in 1958 in Michigan. She went to college to study dance. By age 20, she was singing, dancing, and performing. She had her first hit songs in 1982 and 1983. Her album *Like a Virgin* launched her to superstardom in 1985.

The singer became known for her edgy performances. She came to represent female power in the 1980s and 1990s. Her music described a woman who was in charge of her life. Her work pushed the boundaries of pop music. She paved the way for later stars such as Lady Gaga. By 2008, her success made her the wealthiest female musician.

CONTROVERSY

Madonna has had a complicated relationship with the government in Malawi. Some people accuse Madonna and other celebrities of visiting Africa to make themselves look good. Her organization's plans for building a school fell through in 2011. In 2013, the Malawi president stopped welcoming the singer into the country. But in November 2014, the country's new president welcomed Madonna. He hoped Madonna would continue her charity work there.

10

Number of secondary schools built in Malawi's Kasungu province with funds from Raising Malawi.

- Madonna is a pop superstar and actress.
- She shaped 1980s and 1990s pop culture.
- Today, she raises awareness and funding for health and education projects in Malawi.

Madonna began charitable work in Malawi in Africa in 2006. The country has high rates of poverty and HIV/AIDS. Her organization Raising Malawi improves hospitals and schools in the country. She has also adopted two children from Malawi.

Malawi President Peter Mutharika meets with Madonna in November 2014.

23

SIDNEY POITIER BREAKS THE COLOR BARRIER

Sidney Poitier was born in 1927 in Miami, Florida. He grew up in the Bahamas. His family was poor. He only attended a few years of school. When he was 15, he went to live with a brother in Miami. Unlike the Bahamas, Florida in the 1940s was segregated, or separated by races. Poitier found living there difficult. He left for New York City after less than a year.

Poitier had no money when he arrived in New York. He tried out for the American Negro Theater. But he did poorly the first time. He traded unpaid janitor work at the theater for acting lessons. One night, the lead actor could not perform. Poitier stepped in as his substitute. A director saw him and cast him in his first real role. Poitier's acting career was on its way.

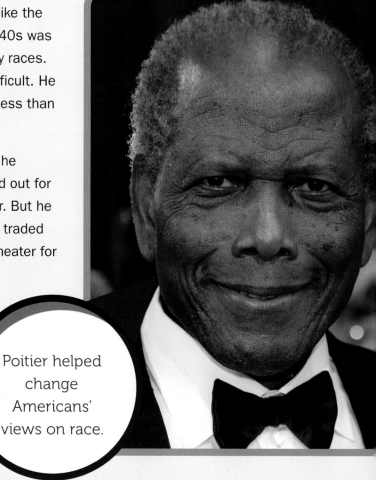

Poitier helped change Americans' views on race.

Poitier's first film role was in 1950 in *No Way Out*. He played a doctor treating a racist white patient. Poitier started choosing stronger and more dignified roles. He turned down parts that reflected society's racist views of black men. In 1964, Poitier became the first black man to win the Academy Award for Best Actor. He broke other racial boundaries in his movies, too. He kissed a white woman in one role. He was engaged to one in another. Poitier showed all Americans that ideas about race could change.

86

Age at which Poitier published his first science fiction novel, *Montaro Caine*, in 2013.

- Poitier is an award-winning actor.
- He took roles that showed black men as strong and dignified.
- He helped break racial boundaries during the civil rights movement.

POITIER IN POLITICS

Poitier has been involved in several political causes. He was a role model during the US civil rights movement in the 1960s. He worked to help the Bahamas become independent from the United Kingdom. Later, he served as the Bahamas' ambassador to Japan. He was also a representative to the United Nation's cultural organization, UNESCO.

OPRAH WINFREY EDUCATES AND UPLIFTS

Oprah Winfrey has been called the world's most influential woman. Her daytime talk show aired for 25 years. More than 40 million viewers watched it each week. Winfrey was the third woman to own a TV studio. In 2011, she launched her own cable network, OWN. OWN stands for "Oprah Winfrey Network."

Born in 1954, Winfrey grew up in rural Mississippi. Her family was poor. But Winfrey went to college. She got a job in TV broadcasting. Viewers loved Winfrey. She quickly moved from local TV to a national show. The *Oprah Winfrey Show* ran from 1986 to 2011. Winfrey became a trusted adviser for millions of viewers. They eagerly followed her recommendations.

Oprah uses her fame to raise money for charitable causes.

Winfrey has consistently used her fame and wealth to help others. Her favorite cause is education. By 2012, she had given $400 million to many projects and scholarships. She built a girls' school in South Africa in 2007. It was one of her biggest projects. The Oprah Angel Network encouraged Winfrey's viewers to donate to charities. The money went to schools, scholarships, women's shelters, and youth centers. It funded projects that uplifted people and improved lives.

$80 million

Amount the Oprah Angel Network gave to organizations over 12 years.

- Winfrey is a TV icon and owner of a TV studio and production company.
- She works to improve education around the world.
- She uses her influence on viewers and others to raise money for charitable causes.

Oprah cuts the ribbon on her new Leadership Academy for Girls in South Africa in 2007.

HOW YOU CAN MAKE CHANGE

Educate Yourself

What cause inspires you? What world issues would you like to see fixed? Talk to your family, friends, and teachers. What are they passionate about? When you decide which causes you are interested in, learn as much as you can about them. Getting educated is the first step in solving a problem. Read books and do research online. Contact organizations that work on the issues. Talk to people who are working on the problems already.

Get Others Involved

Teach people around you what you have learned. Put together a presentation for your class. Write letters to your local newspaper. Call or write politicians in your area. Say what your cause is, why it is important, and what you think people need to do about it. If your cause has a group or organization near you, ask your parent or teacher if you can attend meetings. Get your friends and family members to come with you.

Change Begins at Home

Make a positive change you can see right away by getting involved in your community. Volunteer at a soup kitchen or food pantry. Walk dogs at an animal shelter. Tutor younger kids at your school. There are many ways to help others and make a change.

GLOSSARY

ambassador
The official representative of a country or organization.

empowerment
Giving power to someone or a group, such as women.

envoy
A special messenger or representative.

genocide
The killing of an entire group or culture of people.

humanitarian
Working to improve society and people's lives.

morale
Happiness and satisfaction.

producer
A person who funds and makes movies or TV shows.

protest
Doing or saying something that shows disagreement.

racist
Thoughts or beliefs about a group of people based on their race.

refugees
People forced to leave their homes or countries because of war or political reasons.

United Nations
An international organization that improves relationships between countries and works for peace, human rights, and better living standards.

FOR MORE INFORMATION

Books

Boles, Nicole Bouchard. *How to Be an Everyday Philanthropist: 330 Ways to Make a Difference in Your Home, Community, and World—at No Cost.* New York: Workman Publishing, 2009.

Smith, Roger. *Humanitarian Relief Operations: Lending a Helping Hand.* Philadelphia: Mason Crest Publishers, 2007.

Tougas, Shelley. *Girls Star! Amazing Tales of Hollywood's Leading Ladies.* Mankato, MN: Capstone Press, 2014.

Websites

Do Something
www.dosomething.org

Kids Can Make a Difference
www.kidscanmakeadifference.org

What Can Kids Do
www.whatkidscando.org

INDEX

About the Author

M. J. York is a children's author and editor who lives in Minnesota. She looks to the stars for fashion and gossip—and for inspiration, too.

READ MORE FROM 12-STORY LIBRARY

Every 12-Story Library book is available in many formats, including Amazon Kindle and Apple iBooks. For more information, visit your device's store or 12StoryLibrary.com.